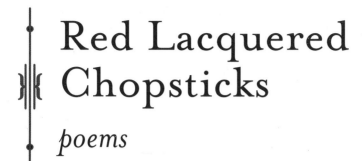

Red Lacquered Chopsticks

poems

BETTY
WARRINGTON-KEARSLEY

We acknowledge the support of the Canada Council for the Arts
for our publishing program.
We also acknowledge support from the Ontario Arts Council.

Cover design by Heng Wee Tan

Author photograph by Jean-Marc Carisse, Ottawa

Library and Archives Canada Cataloguing in Publication

Warrington-Kearsley, Betty, date
    Red lacquered chopsticks / Betty Warrington-Kearsley.

Poems.
ISBN 1-894770-33-1

    I. Title.

PS8645.A773R42 2006   C811'.6   C2006-903081-2

Printed in Canada by Coach House Printing

TSAR Publications
P. O. Box 6996, Station A
Toronto, Ontario M5W 1X7
Canada

www.**tsarbooks**.com

For Michael Anthony Kearsley,

My Champion, Most Critical Critic, and Chaiwalla

Contents

"Remember," my father said, "you are not Eurasian. You are not half anything. You are both English and Chinese. You have inherited the best of both cultures."

Betty P Warrington-Kearsley

Red Lacquered Chopsticks

There's the Anglo-Saxon
who rises in the morning
dressed for breakfast
hankering for kedgeree,
toast, marmalade and tea;
who forces me to sit erect,
spread a napkin on my lap,
use a knife and fork
and keep my elbows
off the table.

Then there's the Sino
who slips downstairs at dawn
in Shanghai silks and kimono,
craving for congee*
with fermented soy,
pickled cucumbers, radish
and deep-fried fish
from a blue-rimmed,
bone china bowl
and red lacquered chopsticks.

There's no telling
who will predominate today;
the one who serves roast beef,
Yorkshire pudding and syllabub,
or the other who stir fries
shitakés with snow peas,
Chinese chives and bok choy,
and contentedly sips green tea.

*Congee, pronounced con-jee, is rice porridge

1

Grandmother's Bed
(from a kampong childhood in Singapore)

Sisters, brothers, cousins—nine of us
side by side on her wide wooden bed
like anchovies packed in parallel lines
on a pale green, grass-scented sorghum mat
from China, that we air each day
in the morning sun.

Grandmother's at one end; I'm at the other,
the rest lie in rank between us,
paternal grandsons before their sisters
then, maternal grandson,
my brother, although younger, she says
is worth far more than I.

Smelling sweet, we climb into our bed
with clean faces, teeth, hands and feet,
claim our coverlets and kapok pillows
and in the dim glow of an old oil-lamp,
settle, as Grandmother cossets close
her youngest and most newly-weaned,

cooing into his darling ears,
love-things, oblivious to grins,
push-and-shove, the odd kick, quarrel, sob,
fisticuffs shadow-boxing on the ceiling
scattering skittish geckoes as they zip along
tonguing quick mosquitoes.

Grandmother lies on a parchment pillow
embroidered with dragons and the phoenix
on black lacquered wood, drum-hollow
and crammed full of dreams from mythic legends,
while ours are puffed with feathers from fowl
she rears to serve upon the table.

She sleeps on no other for fear
that softness may kink or smother.
A foam or feather mattress, she claims,
surrenders the will into its deepness
the way an armchair or a wing-back
wraps itself around the spineless.

Each night I tuck the mosquito net
beneath the mat and trust it holds
them out and me in. I hear their buzz,
slaps as Grandmother zaps them sucking blood
from her precious brood, but more than bites
I fear rolling over and crashing to the floor.

As we gently succumb to slumber,
nine little cousins each next to the other,
some closer, some further from Grandmother
according to our ordained order, how I pray
each night with my heart and head
for a room of my own and a single bed.

Tiger Raid

Grandmother sleeps lightly, always,
the nape of her slender neck nestled
in the saddle of her parchment pillow
and riding pillion, her bone-black hair
tightly-bound and gold-pin gripped.

She rises, reeling, one night
to aberrant squeals and screams
from beyond the guard of household gods,
neighbours and village watch dogs,
rouses her spouse and rushes out,

seizing a pair of poles and torch
en route to the pigpens stopping short,
as suddenly, her broad cone of light
fixes bold, feline eyes—incandescent
between blazes and fiery stripes.

Seething, she descends upon the sties,
more bestial, more beautiful
than the predators and their encircled prey
racing blindly wild-eyed every which way
with white-hot shrieking cries.

Defiant, she stands before the beasts,
clattering clogged feet and pile-driving
her pounding poles into the concrete floor;
cursing words unheard of before
and screeching far louder than the pigs,

until the snarling tigers, awestruck, fall silent
and one by one turn tail and flee
deep into the shadows of jungle trees.
She resettles her pigs, fixes her hair
and, swearing still, heads back to sleep.

4

Grandfather's Pineapples

On his farm behind the house,
beyond the pigpens, hen coop,
and zinc-roofed, honey-pot loo,
between drains for monsoon rains
and the pigs' water-hyacinth pond,
he grows his gold in six raised rows
of super-sized Sarawak pineapples
and daily goes round counting them
for what they are worth in barter
or sweet tender in Japan's Occupation
of Singapore during the war.

Within the ringed barbed-wire run
surrounding his modest plot
a couple are cropped one night;
lopped clean off the stem.
No footprints to be seen, or spoor,
yet the loss of more and more
mature, succulent fruit—

until a worker keeping the kilns,
finds within, a soldier fast asleep
in full battle dress; about him, skins.
He is forgiven for it is 1947
and he, unaware the war has ended.

Going to Market
(Singapore 1950s)

Blazing heat on black umbrellas
roofed against the Singapore sky
we pace our unpaved, pot-holed route
to market at the tenth milestone—
a long trek from kampong Mata Ikan
when you're nearly ten and trotting
beside Grandmother
on her tightly bound size-three feet,
she wishing they were as large as mine.

Are we nearly there? I ask impatiently
as the heat, soaring to midday, draws
unending streams from brow and back.

In ponds we pass, water-hyacinths
with translucent lavender petals
briefly distract, bouganvillea,
abundant with bracts, jacaranda,
frangipani and flame-of-the-forest
canopy the rain-scarred, blood-earth road,
eroding, always, a little more
with each monsoonal downpour,
tapering in places to simple tracks.

We come upon the welcome hum and buzz
of open-air business. I run ahead
of Grandma's cautions: ladies
must never appear to be in a hurry
so please walk slowly, always look cool
and don't disgrace her or the family,
our ancestors or anyone else she may know
although I did not think the dead would care
but would never dare tell her, so
on we plod until suddenly we're there.

Market at the Tenth Milestone
(Singapore 1950s)

The market floor, alleyed and uneven,
is wet from melting ice and muddied
by clogs, coated with kampong soil,
clattering across cracked cement blocks.

Grandmothers in uniform samfu—
sky-blue or white tops frog-buttoned
over black, baggy, cotton bottoms—
lean over fish, freshly caught but not yet cleaned,
still twitching on the slab; and bargain hard
for a kati of this—and pointing—of that;
choicest for the family; cheapest for the pigs.

Mothers in colourful samfu of more flattering fit
with sleeping infants slung across their backs
snap bunched green bean tips for tenderness,
fondle cleaved cuts of flesh and haggle
with the hawker taking flak and shooing flies,
then move on to heckle with another
equally keen to profit by even one lean cent.

Ducks sit ruefully on the hot pavement,
feet trussed, wings flapping as they duly
watch their kind being slaughtered beside them;
a stifled sob gobs my throat.

Day-old chicks and ducklings bob
and chirrup in their baskets, not
knowing which broody mother will care
to coach them in the culture of their kind.

The rising heat pitilessly descends,
drawing from dank earth the putrid
stink of rotten refuse, the stench
of stale urine, of dead and dying kittens

abandoned from birth and lying
beneath a broken, wooden bench.

Scraggy puppies rear sightless heads
from gutters, struggle to rise
on rubbery legs in the drains
where they have been left to drown
in the next prevailing monsoon rains.

Above the drone of general chatter
intones a visiting vendor's call
and crowds gathering here and there
examine and test the latest ware
from kitchen tackle, toenail clippers, tin mugs
from China, to cure-all balms for rubbing in.

There are gunny sacks full of curry spice;
cockles, mussels, oysters, sun-shrivelled
sea cucumbers for arthritis soup;
pickled olives and plums, both sweet and savoury,
dried cuttlefish and squid; anchovies by the scoop,
and eggs aged a hundred years that reek of ammonia,
gluten for vegans, gingko nuts and sesame seed,
aphrodisiacs, ginseng, mushrooms and cordyceps,
baskets of betel chews, tobacco leaves, snuff,
cakes of coconut cattle feed, and crockery
racked on trestle tables with kitchen stuff.

There are coloured ribbons and delicate lace
from Shanghai in piles on a sorghum mat,
and scribes who write letters
for the illiterate or blind—for a small fee,
psychics with amulets, joss, and yarrow sticks
that you toss, let drop and hope for the best
when they read them—and your mind.

And every other day a whining truck,
bulging with bananas arrives, rallying

a rowdy crowd, climbing, reaching
body over sweaty body, seizing
the heavy combs and clusters
of various size and colour and lowers them
to the ground until all are gone
within the hour and the vehicle roars away.

At steaming breakfast stalls
those from afar stand or sit and down
their rapid fill of dumplings, congee,
hot black coffee in glasses, and gossip
between mouthfuls with those they know
from kampongs along the coast,
some whom they do not often see,
and when the sun, now overhead, begins
its searing toll of noon, folks leave,
stalls fold and soon the market
at Tenth Milestone is cleared and dead.

Seahorse

Ping Fatt Lee the apothecary
has a large jar of fine filigree
sun-dried seahorse skeletons
he uses in oriental medicine,
each spiny form, in foetal position,
succumbed in eternal sleep;
Neptune's mythical steeds, once
translucent and ethereal,
riding the watery deep,
plying their piscine tails
in the oceanic ebb and swell
happily minding their own business.

My grandmother who came from China
keeps her seahorses afloat
in sacred oil
on the altar of her ancestors
between candles that drip
and joss that daily renders
sweet sandalwood scent
aloft beyond the rafters
to move the hearts of gods
with countless whispered prayers
for a better life in future years
beyond this one; most of all
to return to the human realm
next time a man, complete,
like the male seahorse
whose belly swells and projects
his progeny of both genders
without remorse.

Foot Loose

When she turned six
foot binders came
with bias-cut strips
to cripple her toes
so they could no longer grow
become splayed or stubby
like those coarse peasants'
in grubbies, barefoot, planting
in muddy paddy fields
or combing golden sandbanks
for cockles and clams.

Only her great toes were coddled
for erotic show: the narrow,
winkle-picker look in vogue
ten centuries, favoured
by the beaded silk-slippered aristocracy.
Racking pain inflamed
each limping pace she took
heel to toe over the hump
of four others buckled back
and trussed beneath each foot,
blue-black and senseless—
for the promise of good looks
and a good husband.

Washing her eighty-year-old feet,
the pads of her 1910 toes
dent her size four soles,
each spooned in a shallow nest,
a niche across an arch that bridged
her six-year-old screams
of pain, and pleasure of foreplay
at sixteen, unbound and freed
by him who desired her best.

Family Menagerie
(according to Chinese astrology)

My mother was a Rat,
a Lilliputian Amazon
with Herculean strength,
of quick wit and temper,
who'd fight ferociously
were her children threatened,
do everything right first time
or lightning impatience
would strike it void. Rats
get on with Monkeys,
like my brother, Dragons
like my sister, and Oxen,
like my husband, animals
they may marry, but not Horses
so she would never live with me
fearing we'd always disagree.

My father was a Tiger,
a six-foot-two size-twelve-shoed
red-headed, moustachioed king
of cats who prowled Malayan jungles
with his Remington 303
for wildlife to carry home
on the well-worn pillion of his Norton
for his beloved, incompatible Rat,
his kittens, and true-blue friends:
Horses, Dogs, Dragons and Boars,
but rarely Monkeys or Serpents.

My brother married a pedigree Dog
when Monkeys, declares the zodiac,
ought to pair with Dragons or Rats,
and run from Tigers and Oxen,
challenging my sister-in-law
who must dodge the Dragon and wed,

instead, Tiger or Horse, or even a Boar
or Rabbit for a better match.

My sister chose a lovely Boar,
best among her array of suitors
of assured rapport: Rats, Monkeys, Serpents,
Tigers and even a few crowing Roosters,
each voicing his ardent passion,
but no, the Dragon lady loved her Boar,
her champion truffle hunter.

And I, ignoring all these signs,
espoused an English Fire-Ox
instead of pet Tiger, Goat or Dog,
and he, his charming Water Horse
against the wisest counsel of elders
to select proposals only
from Serpents, Roosters and Rats,
never from Goat or Horse.

This is why we all have chosen
each to live in separate countries
for distance, often inconvenient,
thickens life-long harmony.

Negative Mother

Dr Jung, don't tell me my problem lies
in having a "negative mother"
although in your view this may not be denied.
You see, poverty drives the desolate to desperation
and Chinese daughters were dispensable then,
as obedient brides, barter for sacrifice. Or slaughter
at birth. Mothers have no need to speak—
you read it in their eyes—that fleeting glance
of pity in the swill of sorrow or shame
and the greater pity of ignorance.
She cannot be blamed, Dr Jung. You see,
it was not her fault she could not write her name,
kindred generations before her could not
do the same, either. Please understand, Dr Jung,
it is only what you describe in her as negative
that drove me, with my compensatory complexes
you call "martyr" and occasionally, "hero,"
to do what I did,
that she, and all her other offspring might live
in common human dignity. You see,
from beginning to end it was a simple matter:
Necessity.

Skin Deep

When I was small and fell
and grazed my knee
my Chaozhou grandmother
would lift me up,
and reciting, comfort me:
tak jik, tak chuq
mi puere, bo mi kut
her ancient mantra infallibly
removing all disaster from me.

A spell, when I was old enough
to know, meant:
every blow, if only skin deep,
not spreading into bone,
always heals, however slow.
It won't destroy
forces of life within, but deploys
all means, securing life and limb.

When I woke and heard the surgeon say:
"I think we've got it all, every bit of it,
the cancer's gone. Move on now and live
life to the full,
this extension that may not have been,"

I rejoiced and felt my grandmother's ditty
pulse beneath those breasts I lost
that saved me.

Five Hundred Times

Which way do they go? The strokes
I'd almost forgotten, it's so long
since I wrote with a brush,
learning, when I was six, to dip
its sable tip in a mortar block
pestled with an ink stick wet
with a little water,
and print my name on squared paper
with a flick of the wrist,
learning that each stroke—
      moved in a fixed direction,
      a single sweep up or down,
      right or left, in straight
      or slanting lines, or dots in a row—
      fluid and even,
that each linked
to form fields, countries with kings
and history not to be forgotten,
running mares with flying manes,
forests and flowing oceans, houses
from "pig" under "roof" and love
from "shelter", "heart", and "friend",
and the characters of my name,
Clear Crystal and Lotus.

Today, my hand poised, wavers,
afraid to ruin the page, wondering
where to begin when my old tutor,
shakes loose my grip
on brush and wrist, and whispers,
Be brave now, daring—like this!
Fourteen sweeps for Clear Crystal,
again for Lotus, neither looking right
the first time drawn. Sheet after sheet
fills hours, daylight slips into night
until the handless brush of a nameless ghost

sweeps effortless strokes and draws
a lotus, fully open and crystal clear, rising
like Excalibur, from its pool
of settled muddy water.

Skull

On the beach at Mata Ikan
where an air-raid shelter stands
open to the hermit crabs
and resting place for fishermen,
a gang of boys laugh, shouting
loudly in their Malay tongue,
running, leaping, roughly kicking,
scrambling in a game of ball
in checkered sarongs, tough bare feet,
gouging sand at every turn.

Red-gold flares of early evening
streak the sky above horizon
and for a moment ochre shores
bathed in pink turn fast to blood,
when, as if to curfew's call
the young men skid to a sudden stop
and head straight off to their kampong,
their foundling football left alone,
netted in dulse and bladderwrack,
bracketed by rock and driftwood.

Waves rippling in the rising tide,
rinse the spherical sutured bone,
swill the grit from two large holes,
caress the jaw and the few teeth in it;
the mandible gone, a long time missing:
before the days of DNA,
before the days of dental records,
before satellites hung among the stars
showering us with incessant chatter
and no one knows whose skull this is,
his name or rank, or number.

Feeding the Ghosts

Where I come from,
in the seventh lunar month
we place offerings at the gates
for Hungry Ghosts strolling by
on their respite
from the invisible realm they inhabit.
We do not invite them in
to scare the living
with their gaunt, stringy necks,
gob-stopped gullets and hollow eyes
trolling for hapless hosts to haunt,
or on whom inflict
a particular mischief or demise.
We leave their leftovers to vultures,
scraggy, feral scavengers, maggots,
and all else that crawls.

but in the fifth lunar month
at Qing Ming, we sweep and clean
the graves of all our ancestors,
press fresh gold paint
into the characters of their names
grooved deep into the weathered marble,
and implore each to accept our offerings:
flowers, candles, incense, foods
they craved in life, red wine and tea,
while the children run off to play
among the neighbouring tombs.
After prayers we take the dishes home,
still ample and untouched, their essence gone
to keep alive those bones long buried there,
whose lineage we share in perpetuity.

Ah Leng's Trishaw

"Tring tring!" Not telephone or door bell
but old Ah Leng arrived at six-fifteen
in his rickety, red, polished-to-a-gleam
Triumph of a trishaw. It was green
last week, before it went pell-mell

downhill toward Rochor Canal
when his handbrakes failed to arrest
although he did his level best
but the police were less impressed
when he rammed their parked vehicle

than with his brandy-fuelled breath
that tailed him to the bottom of the hill
into their signalling arms or, worse still,
into the stench-filled, soupy, canal swill
of dead rats, and possibly his death.

Spared by his Taoist temple gods
and from Singapore's Changi jailers' rods—
again, he reckoned he'd beaten the odds
despite stiff fines and depleting wads

which, said a geomancer he went to see,
would improve with a change of colour—
to vibrant red for good fortune rather
than green, purple or any pretty other,
and new brass bells for better *feng shui*.

So I'm off to school in a raging-red trishaw
while Ah Leng pedals in a rapid dash
between dense traffic to miss puddle splash—
his double-bell ringing almost all the way
to get me there on time if not before.

Then he's off again with a wave and grin
to dazzle Aussie tourists on a thrilling spin.

Bidadari
(Bidadari cemetery, Singapore, 2001)

At Bidadari the Christian dead
repose no longer in tranquillity
below their monsoon-mottled marble tombs,
stone angels with moss-grown faces,
fingers wrapped round rosaries missing beads,
and tipsy crosses dropping shadows
beneath the noni trees' full blooms.

No longer does the noble Gurkha, at regimental pace
in sweat-drenched shorts, white Adidas,
daily pound his rhythmic beat
on paths between the dead;
nor novice monks in slate grey robes,
who sat cross-legged on tombstones,
come here to meditate on death,
nor do the poor children with nowhere else to go,
come here any more to laugh and shout and play.

The government no longer cares
who's buried there, not even their own,
discounting countless citizens of the commonwealth,
prisoners of the occupation,
the March '54 air crash victims—and my father—
because, they claim:
there's no land left for building;
the living need their Lebensraum; and
another rail-line underground—
so why support the untaxed dead?

Fifty years he lay in wet, yellow loam
beneath self-sown, overgrown grass;
his uninsured headstone often stolen by graveyard crooks.
Only a number on half-buried paving at the foot
now claims him as our own.
Who knew what we would find, what remains—

21

but fragments of his mahogany coffin—mostly rotten;
within, a bit of shin, part of his crown
and his tarnished name in brass,
nothing more.

Job's Serpent

If he could speak, I would ask:
what has this dutiful Confucian
done to merit this paralysis
that binds him to his bed?
Sparing only face and neck.

Arms and legs fold to his centre,
fixed, like those of a fossil foetus.
Fingers, knotted fists on bent wrists
holding no longer bowl or chopsticks,
clench his mind with a warrior's grit.

His shrunken trunk and sinews
once heaved and flung, nonstop,
hundred-weight gunny sacks
of copra onto his fleet of trucks,
hooked and stacked
by barebacked Chinese crews
chanting ancient shanties
the way fishermen hauling nets still do.

If I could take him on a tour
of all he has missed in Singapore
in this last quarter century, I am sure
he would feel more stranger than citizen
marvelling, wide-eyed, in wonder and awe
at the city-state risen in steel and concrete,
avant-garde architecture, sculptured horizons
pan-island flyovers—airborne, underground
mass rapid transit, and neon, speed and glitz
on all those asphalt roads to the Future.

Night and day, maid Maria-Lynn tends him,
declines time off for fear her living may disappear
without her being there to prevent his passing.
Carefully, she cleanses him, each crevice and fold

as though her own. She knows each scar, each mole
a star in a constellation from heaven;
checks his skin for tell-tale pale necrosis
and swabs his mouth with glycerin. He smiles
as she rinses his scrotum and his penis, and I wonder
if he relives his midnight joys, lusty pleasures
of fabled Dragon and Phoenix
with his late wives and lovers. And I wonder
if she thinks of her husband back home
in the Philippines, four offspring she has not seen
in years since she came to serve in Singapore
in order to feed, clothe, school and afford
them a life transcendent to her own.

He struggles to open one eye, parts the other,
blinks in slivers of light, turning the dim
cataract clouds before him to defining shadows.
He responds wordlessly to questions,
laughs without sound, attempts to lift his head,
shakes or nods in emphasis or protest.
The rest of him, it seems, is gripped,
if not by unpleasant dreams
then by living nightmares—when suddenly
I see his god,

Madre de Tierra, the mythic giant serpent
encircling the whole village of him, sidling in
at the foot and working up,
wrapping her firm, embracing skin round his trunk,
hugging him like a beloved child in the fold
of its mother's arms, gently caressing him;
banding his chest, coil after pressing coil
with barely a cleft; gliding higher and higher,
lovingly cosseting, ebbing his breath
until soon, he succumbs to his shackled desire,
closes his eyes and lets her spreading jaws
swallow his misery whole.

I often wonder what goes on within his mind
as he lies there, silently sleeping
or staring, wide-eyed, at the ceiling, oblivious
to the passing hours, days, months, years
of diurnal ennui and nocturnal dreaming.

And when I hear that rattle in his throat,
I hold my breath, listen
to the bubbling in his chest, the failing cough
and stifled cries as Madre quietly sighs
and gently hugs his wheezing breast into silence.
Yet no one speaks of death.

Tea Merchant

From lacquered tins,
embroidered bags
collared with tea-leaf tags,
and lead-lined drawers
that wall his store,
he offers samples
of steaming greens, whites,
roasted reds and blacks, pure or infused
with ginger, jasmine, lemongrass
or ginseng to redeem balance
of Yin and Yang.

The slippery feel
of grassy leaves, uplifting
whiff of high mountain mists,
cloud drifts and soft rains sealed
in each hand-picked,
mini, thin veined tip
with names that float from his lips:
Lung Ching, Chunmee, Pi Lo Chun.

Bai Mu Dan pearls
from this Spring's first-snow pickings,
fingertip-rolled round petals of jasmine
slowly unfurl, greening
his kettle of clear well water,
each sip unhinging
in that first, stilling cup of tea.

Rooster

My little rooster gathers colours
from black soil beneath bushes
of red and yellow hibiscus,
from flecks of mid-morning sunlight
sipping last night's dew;
the blue and golden corn he feeds on,
comet tails that score the midnight sky
and from rainbows dropping in
after rain in late afternoon.

Before he settles for the night
I lift him from his perch
and cuddle him a little. Each evening
he coyly tilts his head against my chest,
listens attentively and comments
in his own reassuring, condescending way,
the way a priest does in the confessional.
I tell him about my troubled day,
and because a Bantam always speaks
in an especially tender, loving way
I feel absolved from all my suffering
and peacefully leave him to his sleep.

At first hint of dawn, each morning
he comes to the narrow sill
beneath my window, his scarlet cock's comb
stiff as a stunning Mohawk cut.
Then, as if to a choral conductor's cue,
he throws his head back and begins to crow
all the way down from crown to toe
until every shuddering feather of him,
from pore to tip, puffs up
and crows and crows and crows.

Feeding Frenzy

"... in Hefei, China. The tigers' mother...is unable to produce enough milk so
the zoo keepers found a dog to act as a wet nurse."
—*The Ottawa Citizen*, May 2005.

Recumbent in postpartum ease,
she floats between dream and sleep,
two tiger cubs fumbling at her teats
in line with her own pups;
all nose and still too young and blind
to see their difference, or begin
to know the scent of fear, the quivers
that distinguish prey from predator.

In another snap, shot two years ago,
a tigress in a zoo suckles six orphaned piglets,
licking each, between her own,
from snout to toe, blissfully oblivious
to their pale pink, thinly bristled skin
and stripeless, non-feline features.

Even longer gone, a fabled she-wolf
wet-nursed two human infants:
Romulus, eponymous founder of Rome,
and his brother, Remus.
A woodcut shows both on their knees
grasping her swollen, dripping breasts
with podgy little hands, thickly-curled
upturned heads and pursed lips.

There was a time when Boris Yeltsin,
travelling alone on a train
with his infant daughter, frantic to quell
her hungry whimpering, unbuttoned his shirt
and fed her with his embryonic nipple.
In China, child Emperor Pu Yi's wet nurse
kept her milk dripping for him,
cosseting his nine-year whim,

nurturing the unspoken—signals given
in body language that cannot be mistaken,
like one particular sound in the barrier-free
spectrum of music that makes us sit up and listen:
a needy bleat or cry of the nascent tugging,
from primeval depths, our common drive
to kindle the slightest pulse of each new life.

Gansu Foundling
—for Sheila and David Jenkins

A tiny headline in the *Jinchang Times*:
"Another New-Born Girl—Abandoned."

She closed the door and slippered through
the silent, arm-wide Gansu streets
between the growing, midnight hours,
dawn's slivered light
and the first cock's crowing;
past the city's feral hounds
hunkered down in dust, dozing,
without a sound, only a whimper
from the bundle firmly bound
about her waist, beginning to stir
with her quickened pace
to the place where hope lay;
before daybreak,
before local folk or knowledge woke,
before her heart, bloated with anguish,
broke.

She laid her infant at the gates,
and stayed a while that April night
to invoke the gods,
good fortune's smile
through stinging tears
that sopped her sleeves, blurred her sight
while swollen breasts with their copious flow
beneath her camisole, grieved
for the child who would neither grow
in her own mother's arms
nor know the bond of her blood and soul;
an infant conceived against the one-child law,
mis-gendered,
too poor or with congenital flaw,
condemned to death at first breath

from the womb, swiftly snuffed
and thrust
into earth's consuming, indifferent tomb.

As she left, her heart-wracked cries
cracked the air. A prayer
and blessing for her infant's welfare
and for her own reparation
and ability to bear, life-long,
the irrepressible yearning
to know who or what the little one
she bore will become,
she, who to her own mother
will forever be unknown,
and somewhere in the heart of Canada
her pleas are heard by a childless pair
and answered.

Cold

—for Florence Heng Seng Noi, the child in Singapore

Deep into its freezing shroud
it draws me;
a little death
to bury myself in,
in silent keep
beneath these bare-boughed trees.
A child once asked: "Tell me,
how cold is it in your country?"
I replied:
"The snow you walk on squeaks,
and every word you speak
turns to ice,
crashes down,
and shatters in shards
on the frozen ground
splintering
in sharp, syncopated sound."

Winter's Last Fling

End of April, almost;
it shouldn't still be snowing. Not
when spirea along the garden trail
are about to spread their bridal veil;
starry buds ready to burst
into annual bloom now buried
instead, and doomed
beneath a mantle of fallen snow
forecast just yesterday

unbelieved by all until it came,
a few drizzling flakes at first
expected to turn to rain but no,
down it came and began to blow
round and around, swirling snow
with nowhere to go but to and fro,
finally recapping just-thawed grounds,
felling daffodils duped by last week's heat,
flattening new tulip crowns,
spinning narcissi silly in a watery sun,
cropping late crocuses, freaking philodendrons
creeping outdoors far too soon
and freezing sap in succulents
like the cactus moon.

It shouldn't still be snowing,
not when mourning doves,
robins, redwings, cardinals
and even common sparrows
are all puffed up, not from cold
but undoubted inklings of lust, gathering
tufts of shrivel on hedgerows, strands of hay
blown here and there, clumps of dog hair,
a length of string found somewhere,
felt flown from a dryer, styrofoam chips,
wind-strewn news' flyer strips, woolly bits,

a few new pine cones—anything
to cosy a home for nestlings soon due,
so it shouldn't be still snowing this late in spring
and wrecking everything.

Celebrating Tulips

From tour buses crowds pour
into Ottawa and flood the narrow paths
that stream between the oxbow beds
springing another million tulips
from the Netherlands.

Cameras point to the *Presidents*:
crimson *Eisenhowers* shoulder to shoulder
clinking cups with the carrot *Kennedys*.
They pan the *Pompeian Red Emperors*
in a field of *White Dreams*, and *Queens
of the Night* in purple flirting
with frilly pink *Fiestas*
next to golden *Appeldorns*.

Foot-worn visitors crouch and snap
themselves among their full-cupped hosts,
posing in their radiant company
of relative transience,
their momentary ecstasy clicked
in a flash for posterity.

Old Tulips

I love cut tulips best when they are old;
when they continue to grow long and wanton
in a bowl of fresh water
independent of bulbs and soil,
when they stretch and reach in all directions,
tangle and twist
and resist all rearrangement.

I love cut tulips best when they are old;
when their cups begin to spread wide open,
shamelessly display an iridescent core
and on each petal a fuzz patch near the centre
that bees, when they enter, brush their feet on.
And when they turn frail and papery thin
the slender veins that striate their skin
shrivel and frill and tissue them
until, one by one, they begin to slip;
then is each complete
with its pistil and swollen stigma tip
still dripping with a sticky sap
that I had earlier hand-dipped
in pollen and gently tapped,
first one, then the next
that it not miss its final thrill
of sex.

Beaver Dams

I like to think of Castor's dam
as a huge, plump pillow in a water bed
or a fluffed-up feather duvet drawn,
on a cold night, right up over his head
as he hunkers down in woodland floods,
bull-rushed and soggy bogs floating
with a few felled logs, crudely tooth-sawn,
tugged or tumbled in to rot,
and wept on by willows.

Castor cannot help but gnaw
these trunks or else, grows teeth so long
nothing crosses those closed, portcullised fangs;
he either starves to death or succumbs
to a punctured skull or lungs.
So he downs them all on coursing currents,
jams them up on walls of rocks
and wattles and daubs them all with mud.

In his fluid real estate
and cabin built with a woodsman's skills,
he raises a growing extended family
that every farmer fires on
for dwindling streams to their crops.
But one day soon when water's scarce,
droughts increase and normal stores deplete
we may be grateful to the beaver
for his civil engineering feat,
conserving pocket reservoirs
and rich preserves of peat.

Intrusion

He flew in the open door
rousing a draft of wind
making it flap in panic
about my head
forcing me up
to show him the way out
was no different than the way in.
He blindly continued
on his frenzied path,
beating the still air,
wingspan full out
and speeding in all directions.
I followed, at eye level
to the slanting afternoon light,
sight of familiar treetops
from the uncurtained window
where he clung, clawed to the screen,
the look in his yellow eye wild, hopeless.
Suddenly he released everything dark inside him
over the white sill
while I stood watching it
dribble down the wall and splatter
on the glossed wooden floor.
Carefully cupping my hands
around his pounding heart
and laboured breathing,
I spoke to him in gentle human
that even a grackle might understand
and took him to the open door
where he shook his feathers
and soared.

Monarchs
(Danaus Plexippus)

Like petals flung high, fluttering
in the northern sky, clouds
of red and marigold windowed
in black-veined wings—butterflies
with white spotted trim
giving winter the slip,

like the fifty murderous daughters
but one—of king Danaus of Argos,
fleeing for their lives after killing
their intended husbands
on their wedding night.

Or like resurrected spirits
of fallen Aztec warriors, brilliant
in their Monarch battle dress
soldiering on to central Mexico,
gathering in forests
of pine and eucalyptus
in El Rosario, arriving
always in time
for the Day of the Dead

Cardinal

Mid Fall—
this morning the river is steaming
as sluggish dawn shrugs off
her eiderdown sky.
The idle air, already close, drags
into the open window

> the roaring soar of breakfast planes
> rumbling rubber on asphalt highways;
> hiss and groan of three-ton trucks
> gasping painfully to a stop,
> and panicking ambulance sirens

that suddenly cease
as the finally mastered song
of a virgin cardinal,
practised all summer long,
proudly scatters the air.

Migrating Geese

In stubbled corn fields they gather
gleaning furrowed grain,
brown bodies jostling
shoulder to shoulder,
their smooth backs bowed
like Snowbird squadrons
on the ground refueling
before taking to the skies.

When the signal ripples
through their ranks they lift their heads,
shift and regroup, dip their tails
and with a kick-start raise clouds of dust
and spinning chaff they quickly clear
and rise above;
a fleet of white bellies silver in the sky,
an engine of wings beating the wind
to a hum in gaps between cackling,
cruising at altitude, leaders at the nose
skilfully manoeuvering echelons
on changing currents off and on
across countless miles

Oil Patch

Because
those mechanical workhorses
riding the prairie horizon
keep bucking up and down,
whose pistons pump and siphon
tropical flora and fauna
buried millennia underground;

because
flares beacon the bleak night sky
from every site
and pipelines advance their global might
across continents and oceans,

we
fuel the world,
lubricate the hinge on which it spins;
call on countries we've never seen or even heard of
at the touch of a button;
e-mail aunt Eva three times a day so she isn't forgotten
and rev our lives up with everything instant.
We heat the winters, cool the summers,
mill the wind to bake our daily bread;
spread thin films iridescent as dragonfly wings
on surfaces of ponds to snuff the breath
of larval mosquitoes
and make miraculous machines and medicines.

We even go to war for more.

All because
someone once dug up a patch of oil
and when it blew, knew, oddly enough,
that this was no ordinary soil.

Canadarm

(Canada's robotic arm in space)

From cramped confines
in the hold, it bursts—
a mantis limb—unfolding slowly,
joint by joint, in zero gravity;
with bones of crystalline carbon,
golden copper nerves and muscles
ruggedly drilled and wrought,
motoring the unknown, unmapped
intergalactic highways of space,
outreaching the arm of the astronaut.

After more than fifty missions
and seven thousand Earthly orbits
exploring our shoreless universe,
it may, one day, prod even further,
beyond a host of unnamed stars
and re-bond the broken frame of God.

Inukshuk

They are not ghosts who stand—alone
or in silent, familial rows—stark
across the snow-swept Tundra.

Nor are they scarecrows—trapped
in an arctic blizzard, frozen to stone
in ice-capped barrens—but residents
towering with arms held wide,
welcoming as beacons in the dark.

> I once dreamed of Jesus, dying on the cross.
> Climbing up, I carefully took Him down,
> held his blood-cloyed head against my breast,
> my cheek against his crown. When I woke
> He was gone; about me vast emptiness

and saviours of rock and stone
who appear suddenly in the wilderness,
pointing the way home for those lost
on foot, sled or boat, or to a cave,
or lake where fish bite, caribou graze,
or warn where not to go.

They are not ghosts who stand—alone
or in silent, familial rows—stark
across the snow-swept Tundra
but witnesses in stone from long ago.

The Basement

This is where I store
all spare thoughts and memories
silenced and carefully repressed
in neat little packages, padlocked
and placed in tight compartments
for future reference;
shelves of hand-stitched virtues
I have since taken down or ditched;
cupboards crammed with deadly sins
and, for good measure, a few more thrown in
you never know when you may need again
for a bit of pleasure or when you run out
of regular ammunition and want to draw
on the big guns for ego defence and survival.
These are labelled "Poison."
In case of overindulgence
dial 1-800-Confessional.

Yet, I have questioned, lately,
the use of all this
when what I truly desire is less of more,
more of less, and no excess baggage
to weigh me down.
Only I didn't know it then,
not until those ageless inhabitants
I meet in archetypal dreams
including some I hold in high esteem
who often slip new pictures in my head,
suggested: the art of living in bliss
begins when all that's left is emptiness.

Hope

Never more present than at weddings.
It is
in the heart and in the air.
Grasped in the smiles and handshakes.
In light unleashed from darkest eyes.
Cupped gently in hands at prayer.
It echoes in the peal of bells,
their timbre lin-g—e—-r—-i——n————g.

It ascends in the swinging incense
floating aloft to embracing arches.
Swells in the jubilance of unstoppered organs.
Hovers in the pitch and drop of voices
and in soft wafts of whispering.
It diffuses in floral auras,
from roses buttonholing lapels.
Fills the heart's emptiness,
and is eloquent in silence.

It lies in the dreamy-eyed glaze,
the longing of mother and grandmother,
the gaze of bride and groom exchanging vows,
the rings they place on each other's fingers,
and in the awe of their union.

It rings in the crystal clinking in toast;
in speeches and testimonials;
in the laughter of abandoned sorrow,
crunch of icing bricking the cake
young children cram in their mouths.
It floods the full, dripping breast of a mother
nursing her newborn infant.
It whips the blood in the hip-hop, clap,
bopping to upbeat drums and the sax.

Hope flies to another in the fling of her bouquet

with every good wish it carries,
and leaves with the radiant husband and wife
beginning their new life, "Just Married."

Pomegranates

Standing by the market stall
in the fullness of her term she watches
my hands grasp and roll each globe,
fingering the ruddy blush
for blemishes against the taut, leathery skin
ensuring its gravid load within, secure
from where it came off the stem
to its sealed pore at the other end.

Weighing one against the other
on mental scales I spread and press
my thumb across each rise of bump,
each pit of hollow
when suddenly, beside me, a jump;
she apologizes, says: *oh*, and strokes
the shifting bulge beneath her robes.

Happy Birthday

You would have been eighty-eight
had you lived to celebrate this day.
These many unhappy returns bring thoughts
I've often pondered; our revised fate;
how life would have been
had you not died
and, as the padre told me in those days,
gone straight to heaven.

It might have been different, but who's to say?
Mama was left with debts unpaid;
squeezed her blood blue simply to live.
She never asked why, just did.
That's life, she said,
better to get on with it;
won't do any good to whine.

Your eternal life then lived itself in mine,
its ghostly, slow-grown discontent,
determined purpose and intent—
sometimes hard to define
whose will it was, yours or mine
that drove me on beyond my primal fears
to finish unspent business you left behind

until I could no more go on. Until one day
I woke up, lost, uncertain, empty of self,
having been driven all these long years
the driver had suddenly gone.

Origami Lovers

Thank you for the card, she said. It was very kind
but you shouldn't have. It really wasn't necessary.
After fifty years I'd rather forget and often wonder
why I agreed to relinquish myself,
becoming now what marriage has made of me—
no one should expect to be married this long. I wish.
Believe me. I've seen my individuality gone, like sugar
slowly dissolving in a cup of tea—grown cold,
dark and bitter; the woman I thought I was sold
in deluded youth. Now I'm old I clearly see
what the matter is: I've matured much more, it seems,
than he, in all these years we've been married.
I regret the bleeding years life's taken from me—
for him, the children, grandchildren and home;
most of me gone, and I become alone
as the separate bed I now sleep in.
The wedded bliss of marriage came, went, wasn't.
Now I wonder how all this time was spent
nurturing everyone except myself like the proverbial cow—
expected of my mother before me, of hers before her,
etcetera. What's worse is I've become his. Mothering
is what women do best they said or assumed,
and don't you show any hint of unhappiness! It's disloyal.
That's my generation; unconfessed delusions
gobbed in their hearts til they burst and wept
deep, sorry sobs into their pillows in the dark.
He never says much now, unmuttered thoughts
tight in his head. What is there left, except death
for an elderly couple so separate in companionship;
together yet apart, for this is how we are
even as years roll on and he now calls me 'Mom'.
I've even lost my name. But you're so very kind
to wish me a happy golden anniversary
with many more the same. Never! I mean
never mind and oh, please forget what I've just said.

It really is a beautiful card; the nicest yet
I've ever seen: Origami lovers—in kimono
of purple silk, orange blossoms and green umbrellas,
such rich material—gorgeous colours and they, regal
as we were that surreal day so long ago, when it never
occurred that love could one day cease. Again, thank you.
I shall frame your card and place it on the mantelpiece.

Negligée

Who knows what lay in his head, she said.
He slept in his quarters upstairs, kept
to his own business. I minded my own,
and lived below with my two spaniels.
We met at weekends when he came home,
being away Monday through Friday.
I hardly saw him even then; never
at breakfast, occasionally at dinner,
for he was always in a rush. Did just
as he pleased, but I, being decades younger,
mostly did as I was told.

We had grand balls and garden fêtes. I recall
the silver, Royal Doulton, glittering crystal.
To this day I can still hear our hired hands say
what a fine time was to be had here, for sure!
Which pleases yet saddens me when I think
back to when they sweated in the kitchen,
churning butter from cream cooled in the well,
roasting game on the spit and serving canapés
to his guests but wouldn't be allowed a tip.

You see that boat in the bay? That's the Choy Lee
he bought and named after me immediately
we were married. Elderly now and on my own
I should have sold or given it away but couldn't;
like this brand new negligée I bought especially
to stun him in bed the evening he returned
from two weeks conferencing in Florida,
thinking it would have pleased him
when he walked in with an American blonde
clinging to his arm, and said:
Meet my new woman—Florence.

Fishnets

The lingerie in her drawers
came from a generation past.
Wear what you can, she had asked
in her last request. I lifted each,
crinkly-soft in their tissue wrap
and sniffed—the clean-skin scent
of alkanet each time I kissed her.
Then I felt, at base, a hand-sewn case
of black lace suspender belts
and French fishnet stockings,
streamlined with walk-away seams,

finely designed with butterflies
flying tandem from the ankles up,
spreading their wings wide
when I tried them on. Some, styled
with slender serpents sinuously hooked
round the thighs, slithered down
with lascivious smiles, tongues flicking,
and I imagined their skinny, limbless torsos
shimmying with every pace she took.

What would Adam have said
had he met Eve, not only in these
but mesh cut-out bras, fingerless gloves,
microplunge panties, come-on ultras
like a Leopard's Legacy mini G-string,
Purple Python Double-D bikini top,
spotty, chic Brazilia Bottoms, Passion's
Fancy Extra Tummy-Tuck Pantyhose,
a classic thong? Or stick-on Fig Leaf?
But innocent Adam, wouldn't know.

And I wondered if Flora had worn these
decades before she was ninety,
or were they bought for fantasy play

when a hot flush of lust overwhelmed,
that made her doff her clothing and skinfit
herself in spandex fishnets; a mermaid
willingly caught in a fisherman's fling
with her six-inch, sling-back stilettoes
well dug in, and he, helplessly pinned,
loving every minute of it.

Rush-hour Interlude

Turning left on Bank, I slow,
a driver ahead slams his brakes,
damming a line of fidgety cars
as an elderly woman, weighed low
by long years, steps from the curb
and edges into the grit-blown road,
white cane in one hand,
billowing bags in the other;
unrushed or bothered
following her staccato tap-tap
fumbling its zig-zag way
across the street.

Her blowing navy blazer
of psychedelic stripes
hypes her hot-pink trousers
checkered electric blue,
newly bought on "Special"
from nearby Value Village,
tags intact and flapping.

Her head loudly sports
a purple paisley scarf
windsocked by autumn gusts.
Tap-tap, tap-tap, tap-tap
she briefly stops midway
and stares, unfocussed
for what seems hours
in a timeless gap, then ambles on,
her sightless path clear;
smiling, all the while, to herself,
and I wonder if it's a measure
of gratitude for the zebra pedway,
or some other private pleasure
creasing her weathered face.

House for Sale
—for Kveta Brandesj

Driven deep into the lawn,
the "For Sale" sign sent tremors
through the foundations
of her thirty years on the crescent.
She never knew it would come to this
quite so soon, she said, recumbent
in her old chaise longue
she now depends on as day bed
in the otherwise unused dining room;
seeming surprised, at seventy-nine,
how set ways can suddenly change
from a comfortable, calendared routine
that could go on forever
to the intrusion of a future
she had only read about
in insurance ads for the aging
and optimistically tossed out,
not noticing
the fine print in her joints,
the need to raise the hem of pants
longer now than when she bought them,
the wider shoes that bucked against
her innate sense of fashion,
the crumbling backbone
giving way when she tried to shift a stone
in her increasingly rampant garden,
making it awkward to rise or walk
without the indignity of a walker
or weed without a kneeler;
a state she believes unusual
for one who had weathered all
in pre- and postwar Europe.
She weeps for the rift that severs
assignments in her head
from her body's fulfilling,

and wonders
if only, if only she might have seen
the daily kinks, the twinges that signal
wear and tear of her inner machine
and had not so stoically ignored them,
whether she could have unwrinkled them
and forestalled the inevitable.

The Move
—for Kveta Brandesj

As the U-Haul draws away
she strains to look behind
at the empty house
no longer home,
"SOLD" slapped across the sign
on the rusty-leafed lawn.

"The upheaval was hell,"
she says, apologetic
for the four-letter word
she now allows herself,
unconstrained, at eighty.

"But the penthouse floor
I'm going to
is nearer heaven,
with its panoramic views
of the river, the Gatineaus
and sugar maples turning colour
before their sap runs dry."

Estate Sale

Like hyenas closing in
after the kill they enter,
draw close, sniff around
and tear apart, room by room,
her body of belongings,
flipping bone china
from Limoges, flatware, souvenirs
from trips home to Norway,
her great-grandmother's underwear
exposed in a leather trunk,
crocheted and neatly folded;
lace trim, collars, clothing
long past vogue, lambskin coats,
mink stoles, dead-alive with paws, tails,
narrow heads and gimlet eyes.
Bric-a-brac in a musty basement,
Ibsen's *Collected Works* in Norwegian,
Thor Heyerdahl's *Kon Tiki*, LPs
and cigar boxes, wigs on a closet shelf,
shoes to challenge Imelda Marcos;
a host of paintings, and a photo:
a nurse with a kindly face
in her prime—herself perhaps,
in cap and pinafore; eyes
following all around, watching
the unkindly way the living
finger and pick over the dead.

Twilight
—*for Charles Fisher, Juan O'Neill, and Judith Anjowski*

Often on a broken night
between the shortening winter dark
and lengthening spring light,

our venerable elderly quietly slip
the skid and slither of thawing ice
on their last, long trip,

leaving their empty bodies behind,
abandoned baggage of a lifetime
and Farewell cards unsigned,

and when what is thought or said
of them, they return—as they were then,
in a flash—alive again from the dead.

Enid's Ashes
(Little Qualicum Falls, BC)

Not into the onslaught of waters
raging through this gorge,
nor into their thunderous swell,
felling loose boulders down,
down between deep crevices
of black, stalwart rock
where firs and cedars on top
claw tight-clung roots that drop
a mile or more below
to where the homing salmon leap,
gull and crow gather;
where the wild, wet moss
slathers in streaks,
and slivered light peeks
from shade and shadow.
Not there,

but here,
in the rainforest, among evergreens
aspiring to the skies,
spritzing the air with healing,
embracing wind in storm or breeze,
confiding in clouds enshrouding them,
whispering into swirling mist
and quelling loud rainfall on infant trees
busy sapling in log nurseries;
preserving all, and not least, the peace
that comes from hugging silence.

Here, between bursts in the winter sky
overcast but for a moment dry
we dribble her ashes in a winding trail
between bracken, ferns, salal and all
other undergrowth, the pale white line
slowly sinking in the plump forest bed
of cedar and pine.

The Send-off
—*for Colonel Patrick Stogran*

Reading the *Ottawa Citizen* tonight, I wept
farewell to four Canadian paratroopers
killed—not by foe—but "friendly fire"
at the ghoulish hour of two a.m.
Who knows what occurred in Kandahar;
it's anyone's guess on harsh terrain,
an unlit stage, and in the wings, Death
prompting elemental fear in all
no matter how well-trained when,
with gob-stopped breath beneath their gear—
guns flared, cracking fear's soundless tread
when overhead, a Falcon pilot, hyped
suddenly loosed his laser-guided quarter-ton,
declared in self-defence. The Pentagon
regrets the tragic loss of allied lives, of course—
but no remorse—it's a game, after all—called War.
It choked me most:
not when regimental comrades of the four, bore
their coffins before coalition and their own
in ceremonial send-off from a floodlit bay;
not at the midnight lament of the bugler's *Last Post*,
nor even when unchecked tears traced each face
unabashed, more resolute in *esprit de corps*
as the flag-draped cortège slowly filed past
and slipped the four, one by one onto the plane,
but when
their supreme jumpmaster and Commander,
drew back a tear, stood to attention,
and tapped each casket as he did each trooper
before that awesome leap into the unknown.
It was his way, strange as it seemed at a time like this:
that friendly slap on the shoulder, brother to brother
or sister, to assuage fear, reassure
that nothing changed in life from yesterday
and share with each a last moment alone to say:
"*You're OK, Jumper. Have a good one.*
You're airborne!" Going home.

Jacques' Funeral

(in memory of Brig Gen Jacques Morneault)

After solemn High Mass and Requiem Eternam,
the plaintive fanfare of the soldier's Last Post
pierced the dome of Saint Léon's
gilded frieze of Latin prayers,
frescoed hearts of angels and of saints above,
of broken mortals' in their pews below
and the casket in which he was laid to rest—
he departed

to crackling volleys of rifle fire,
the platoon from his very own
le Royal Vingt-deuxième Régiment,
Cinquième Groupment du Combat,
come all the way
de la Base des Forces Canadiennes, Valcartier.
They,
white-gloved, groomed and polished,
stooped to swiftly gather
the shiny, runaway casings
and gave them
to the scrambling children.

Obsession with Time
—for Michael Parkin

The face of grief in a hollowed clock
mourning the loss of time;
a narrow, fine-boned skull owned,
once, by a living red fox;
a weasel's femur, foot of a mouse;
remnants of other lives snuffed out,
dug up, found and hung
from a sun-bleached antler
on pendulum lines marking
the inevitable erosion of time;

a solitary, crimson rose
stark in its place on the base
of crinkled memory;
in a papier-mâché box, keepsakes
of an ancient coin from the Orient,
an oak leaf from northern woods
in autumn, perfectly shaped, fallen
and caught before the rot; a curl
of silver birch bark
and, on the dark felt floor
in a corner of its universe,
a spark of light from a tiny zircon.

In the air a chill, a presage
from clockwork cogs and calipers
measuring and logging, non-stop
Time, Past and Present, swiftly passing
with each run-on tick; the prescience
we get from treasured dead we collect
mining the immeasurable, marvelling
at the matter of their becoming
and of our own unbecoming
in the interminable tug of time.

Eloquence

In a teahouse by the railroad station
where the cone-nosed Shinkansen
bullets on from Ueno to Hiroshima,
two women in persimmon and rose kimono
sit, in conversation;
one, her face a running film of all she says,
is mute to me without her tongue; her hands lie layered
on her lap, not interfering. The other listens,
leaning forward, obi neatly pillowed in her back,
her face reflecting all she hears
but saying nothing. Between sentences
she bows in silent understanding
of the understated or unsaid.
Before she speaks they raise their cups, breathe
into steam, lower their eyelids and sip.
They seem composed as they rise to go
with thoughtful paces deep and slow.

Autumn in Hakone
(Japan)

Flamboyant maples flamenco
all over volcanoes
from Yugawara to Yumoto. Colour-crazed
crowds from far and near
sway on funiculars,
or on foot, coach, or train gaze
in wonder and murmur:
Ah-so? De-s'-ka. Even the slow,
and aided lame boldly trek
their winding upward way to view
this annual arboreal splendour
again, miraculously, turned to flame.

Below us, the ground rumbles
with hidden giants spewing
halitosed fumes of sulphur
in a thick, yellow haze
that stinks daylight out of days
and fumigates subterranean flumes.

Stifling breath, we rise above
Mount Kami beyond Komagatake
over the Valley of Death
and its bubbling fumaroles
that swallow whole the unrequited,
resting their unhappiness.

Down in crater lake, Ashi-no-ko,
white caps and sails race on ahead
the brisk air's embrace,
and somewhere in the stillness
the timbre of a distant temple bell
lingers in the wilderness.

When firey maples bolero

on Hakone's hills and mountains
and golden persimmons lantern
late autumn's leafless branches, pilgrims,
in humbled awe and praise, bow low
and may, sometimes, on clearer days,
glimpse majestic Mount Fuji.

Onsen in Izu
(thermal spas in Japan)

We bow acknowledgement as we slip
into the vapour veil of steaming baths
stripped to our glass biographies.

Beneath the scrutiny of lowered lids
rewritten history is curiously read
from acres of an aging landscape

well weathered to a mature shape,
the way hills round, valleys fill
and scarred escarpments soften

smudged in scented volcanic sludge,
lathered, rubbed and effleuraged
satin; sluiced, sauna'd and soaked

in sweltering subterranean flows
fuelling spas, roadside geysers and blow holes
that spurt from crooks of devils' elbows.

Nothing matters here, it seems. And least, nudity.
Anonymous we are, eery in our surreality,
ghostly shadows—matronly mama-sans, nubile willows

glistening amber smooth in dim-lit fog. There's no difference
between sweating last night's sweetness, iced sake, sashimi
and yesteryear's vinegar and piss in here. Unshed tears,

for unconsummated living, stifled yearnings, fears, years
of neglect, sadness for the nature of things, regret
materialize and torrent down the indifferent windows

looking out to sea. Sweat flows from scalp to toes
in steady streams until, unfettered,
we tenderly nurse our newborn shadows recovered
from the karmic rubble of imperfect dreams.

Snuff Bottles

"Fetch the snuff," Bao-yu commanded, "If snuffing can make her give
a few good sneezes, it will clear her head."
                    —*Dream of the Red Chamber*, CAO XUEQIN

In Manchurian days
before the Regency,
my venerable ancestors,
topknotted and pigtailed,
wore their snuff bottled
in chrysanthemum-carved,
palm-size cloisonné
or lacquered cinnabar jars
hung from their waists.

Sitting at afternoon tea
shooting the breeze,
they would spoon a hit
upon a thumbnail
or web of outspread thumb
and quickly sniff it
up a nostril with a whiff
and shudder loose the stuff
that plugged inertia or their wit
in one almighty sneeze.

Today it is not simply baccy
spiked with pepper and ephedra,
or purest pungent opium
that kept my greats and grands so happy,
but hash, heroin and crack cocaine
that keeps them coming back again
to where the snuff is hidden.

Painting Lotuses
(I-Chen Wu, 1973)

Young Lao-Tzu sits in stillness
before a ream of unrolled rice paper
emptying his mind, annulling himself.

Then with wide wet brush, dips
only its thick edge in the palette
of freshly pestled, dark green ink.

A sweep spreads a single curve
at the base of the page; light and shade
appear, at first without apparent meaning

becoming clear when sturdy stalks rise
from a broad-leafed floating pad,
raising three pink lotuses from mud:

the fading, the fully open, and the new.
Finished, "This is for you," he says.
"Refusing me will ever remain with you."

Konton

(a Chinese/Japanese parable)

In the Beginning was a kindly fellow
named Konton, also known as Chaos,
who lived alone in bliss, happily,

with no eyes, ears, nostrils or mouth
in a head smooth as polished stone,
unlike everyone else. Happily.

Until one day, those he had helped
wished to offer him their gratitude,
so he let them. Happily.

How much happier he'd be, they said, if he
could breathe, smell, hear, eat, speak and see,
and carved a hole a day in his head. Happily.

On the seventh day, at the end of work they said
how pleased he'll be and asked how he felt
but found poor Konton dead. Not happily.

"Is That So?"

(a Zen legend)

When her son was born
the village was aghast—
she was unwed and her lover,
at her bidding, had fled
for fear her father, uncles and brothers
would oust and kill him,
and she, panicked and trembling,
pronounced the father of the infant
none other than Zen Master Hakuin
who lived in his hermitage
deep in the forest, high on the hill.

Clamouring, they stormed
into the sandalwood silence
and thrust the child into his arms,
charging him with its paternity
and of the estranged mother, her ruin.
He listened to their accusing
cacophony of cries and curses
and remained, all the same, unruffled.
And while they awaited his reply,
he carefully scanned their faces
and simply murmured: "Is that so?"
Roused again in protest they chorused,
"Since he is yours, you care for him!"
"Is that so?" he murmured as they left
and held the tiny bundle to his breast.

Not long after, the lovers wed
and yearned the return of the son
they had earlier abandoned,
and on their longing sought the hut
deep in the forest, high on the hill
until, before the Master, they knelt
in repentance and confessed
the child to be their own and their desire
to take him home.
Old Zen Master Hakuin listened
and gently said: "Is that so?"

72

Ties That Bind
(a love myth)

In my loose-toothed, pigtailed days,
Grandmother, steeped in ways
of the Chinese sages,
told me how lovers reached their destiny.

The Goddess of Love, who surveys Earth,
casts her glance on every birth and destines
for each the one to wed
with a spin from her spool of silken thread
divinely dyed in invisible red.

Swift as a loon she swoops way down
from an unseen side of the maiden moon
like a comet streaking a starlight spread
across the nebulous sky
to the cot of a sleeping newborn girl
and deftly ties a promissory knot
round her left ankle, and with a flying kiss,
beams off again to the skies;
her filmy robe an auroral float
streaming close behind.

Transcending time and trackless space
she finds, in a remote or obscure place,
a handsome baby boy and binds
his right ankle with the silken bond
tied to the one whom he will marry.

The Goddess of Love, wise and gracious,
does her best in the human realm
for nuptial happiness, yet
some still blame her for careless error
when matters go wrong, and ardently wish
for a marriage less long, more full of bliss.

She roams the heavens and soars the ether
carrying, always, her red spool with her
else masses of singles will curse their fate
for old age with neither offspring nor with mate.

Sometimes on Earth, multiple births
occur beyond her coping;
without hesitation, she summons her aides
who pair the infants before they run
or are otherwise bound
for the single life, searching in vain
for a husband or a wife.

Should her aides become careless
or unwise sometimes, troubles arise
as silk cords unwind in the race to bind
left and right ankles the whole world over.
Much twisting occurs, entanglements too,
same gender hitching, reefing and splicing,
and knots you never knew could exist;
webs and trellises in parallel or series
that any mathematical genius
clacking beads on his abacus
would take a lifetime to unravel.

North, South, East, and West, chaos unreels
throughout their travels as silk cords cross,
entwining the tortuous paths of lovers
unsuited to each other and mired
in myriad affairs of undesired fate.

This accounts for much in life,
Grandmother said—of why some wed,
why some meet yet never marry;
why some have peace and others strife,
why some loiter and some hurry, hoping
the ever shortening cord will carry

each to the other's destiny.

This is why, my Grandmother said,
the lover's heart knows not the head;
for if it did, it has been led
by the silken cord of visible red.

Red
(from a folk-Taoist point of view)

I.   BIRTH (1896)

Gushed from blood and waters of darkness, Yin
is ushered into candle-lit night and hidden,
like all newborn daughters, forty days
from the brazen grin of Yang sunlight
and his macho, seminal sting. Then,
in mandarin red from crown to toe,
the newly named infant is held to bow
at the altar of ancestors and after, to Tai Yang,
the carnal sun, from whom life flows.
She blinks, bows again, and grows.

II.   MARRIAGE (1912)

She rides to her groom in a palanquin
borne by kinsmen kicking up dust,
spurred by fireworks and sorghum gin.
Her brothers ambush and briskly thrust
the bride beneath a crimson canopy
and race to place her by his side
lest Tai Yang, in his burning lust,
be first to sear her virginity.
Her husband raises her vermilion veil,
impressed she is pretty, fine boned and pale.

III.   DEATH (1980)

He clasps her urn on a scarlet tray
pressed to his chest and leaves the centre
where, each day, they cremate the dead.
Above his head is a large umbrella
shading her lingering cindered Yin
from the finishing stroke of Yang.
In a long, weaving line he and kinsfolk,
heads high, eyes resigned, silently stride
to the newly numbered cinerarium niche
in the ancestral shrine and repository.

NOTES

Red Lacquered Chopsticks, Grandfather's Pineapples, Seahorse, Feeding the Ghosts, Red, previously entitled *Sunstroke, Tea Merchant, Bidadari,* originally entitled *Exhuming Father's Remains* and a number of other poems were shortlisted for the Shaunt Basmaijian Award in 2004.

Grandmother's Bed, Market at the Tenth Milestone, and *Ties That Bind* were first drafted in the village of Telok Mata Ikan in Singapore in 1957.

Feeding the Ghosts: Hungry Ghosts are departed spirits whose insatiable desires in life were impossible to solve (eg. drug addicts). These unhappy spirits, who are said to continue to feed their desires by acts of malevolence and mischief on the living, appear to be appeased by food offerings. Qing Ming (lit. "pure and bright") is known as the Feast of the Dead or the Cult of Ancestral Worship. It is an important festival which falls on the fifth day of the fifth month in the Lunar calendar.

Bidadari was written to commemorate the exhuming of my father's remains in Bidadari Cemetery in Singapore, October 19, 2001. Bidadari was the 37th and largest Christian cemetery to be decommissioned so that "idle land could be turned to profitable use."

In *Job's Serpent* the Madre de Tierra (South American) is a mythical serpent reputed to be large and long enough to encircle and strangle a whole village.

Rooster was co-winner of the Ray Burrell Award in 2004.

Feeding Frenzy was inspired by the *Ottawa Citizen* photo, May 2005, entitled: "Feeding Frenzy—A dog doesn't seem to mind as she nurses two tiger cubs and her own pups at a zoo in Hefei, China. The tiger's mother gave birth Sunday but is unable to produce enough milk so the zoo keepers found a dog to act as a wet nurse."

Gansu Foundling is dedicated to Sheila (MacMillan) and David Jenkins of Ottawa, Canada.

Cold is dedicated to Florence Heng Seng Noi, then a child in Singapore.

Origami Lovers won third prize in the Free Verse Category of the 2002 National Capital Writing Contest for poetry.

House For Sale and *The Move* are both dedicated to Kveta Brandesj.

Twilight is dedicated to the memory of Charles Fisher, Juan (John) O'Neill and Judith Anjowski, who slipped away between January and March 2006.

Enid's Ashes is dedicated to the memory of Enid Kearsley, 1911–2003, whose ashes were scattered at Little Qualicum Falls, Vancouver Is., BC, December 13, 2003.

The Send-off, dedicated to Colonel Patrick Stogran, was inspired by the *Ottawa Citizen* article: "Friendly fire casualties investigated. . .," April 20, 2002. Four PPCLI Paratroopers were killed by a US F16 Fighting Falcon pilot mistaking as enemies the Canadian paratroopers out on a 2 a.m. live-fire exercise. Words quoted in the second last line were spoken by Lt Col Pat Stogran, Commander of the Canadian Forces Contingent in Afghanistan.

Obsession with Time was inspired by Michael Parkin's art exhibition at The Studio in Ottawa, Canada, and his button brooch that read: *'Do It Now! You're Gonna be Dead a Long, Long Time."*

Eloquence merited an Honourable Mention in the National Capital Writing Contest, Poetry Category, May 25, 2006.

Onsen in Izu won the Arc's Diana Brebner Award in 2004

Acknowledgements

In preparing this collection I have made small revisions to several poems. I am grateful to all the publications where they first appeared.

"Skin Deep" first appeared as "All That's Skin Deep" in *Letting Go, an Anthology of Loss and Survival*, edited by Hugh MacDonald. (Windsor: Black Moss Press, 2005.)

"Gansu Foundling" first appeared as "The Gansu Foundling" in *Handprints on the Future, a Canadian Poetry Association Anthology*. (Toronto: Hidden Brook Press, 2003.)

"Rooster" first appeared in the *Grist Mill* 14 (2006.)

"Cold" was first published as "The Cold" in *Tracking Ground, The Friday Circle Anthology Series*. (Ottawa: University of Ottawa, 2004.)

"Monarchs *(Danaus Plexippus)*" and "Migrating Geese" first appeared in *The Delicate Art of Paper Passing*. (Ottawa: Carleton University Press, 2006.)

"The Send-off" was published in *Verse Afire*, Vol. 1, No. 2 (2005.)

"Autumn in Hakone" first appeared in *Bywords.ca*, October, 2003.

"*Onsen* in Izu (Thermal baths in Japan)" was published in *Arc* Vol. 53 (Winter, 2004.)

"Is That So?" first appeared in *Ch'an Magazine*, Vol. 18, No. 3 (1998.)

"Ah Leng's Trishaw" was published in the *Ontario Poetry Society Newsletter*, Vol. 4 No. 3 (2003.)

"Intrusion" first appeared in *Sentinel Poetry* # 35 (2005.)

"Winter's Last Fling" first appeared as "April Snow" in *Poemata, Canadian Poetry Association Magazine*, Vol. 19, No. 2 (2003.)

My infinite gratitude and thanks to:

Michael Kearsley for his indefatigable support—technical and otherwise—continuous supply of cider and encouragement; Seymour Mayne for his upbeat inspiration, encouragement, and energetic and dedicated support as professor and mentor; Armand Garnet Ruffo for his time, patience, and emphasis on the eidetic in creative writing; the late Dr. Jock (John) N. Rushforth, dedicated physician, friend, and mentor; and dear friend Glenys K. Elliott for her personal cosseting while writing at her home on Howe Island.